A Lily Pad
of Possibilities

Fiona Goldsmith

BALBOA.PRESS
A DIVISION OF HAY HOUSE

Balboa Press books may be ordered through booksellers or by contacting:

Balboa Press
A Division of Hay House
1663 Liberty Drive
Bloomington, IN 47403
www.balboapress.com.au
AU TFN: 1 800 844 925 (Toll Free inside Australia)
AU Local: 0283 107 086 (+61 2 8310 7086 from outside Australia)

ISBN: 978-1-5043-2370-3 (sc)
ISBN: 978-1-5043-2371-0 (e)

Print information available on the last page.

Balboa Press rev. date: 12/18/2020

FOREWORD

My niece Fiona has had a brilliant gift of writing poetry since she was a child- a beautiful and different way of seeing life and the world around her. *A Lily Pad of Possibilities* is a glorious selection of her lifetime of inspired works from a life interestingly and well lived.

I love her poems so much that I started posting them on my social media as "Fiona's Friday's" to inspire people in this most surreal and difficult time in our recent history.

You will find much to laugh, cry and smile about as she explores themes we may not have thought of before, in quite that way. Fiona opens your eyes to *A Lily Pad of Possibilities*.

Olivia Newton-John
Aunty O
November 2020

INTRODUCTION

When I was a little lost girl, there were souls who wrapt their arms around the world and cradled my little heart. Even when I was grown there were times when that heart clenched back to child size. Those arms were there with inspiration, wisdom and warm acceptance.

To my dad, Brian Goldsmith the wish weaver... for lighting up my childhood with idealism and looking at the world in a different way.

To my Aunty O who gifted me with acceptance and being a luminous gift of inspiration.

To darling Maria Florio who wrapt me with boundless Italian love from afar and once she knew, she never ever forgot.

To Tasha and Kira for exploding my heart with pride and love and giving me my first taste of purpose.

Thank you to Eve Uittenbosch for illustrations and layout. My brother Brett Goldsmith for my head shot, Sarah Newton John for editing, Simone Hanning for support and inspiration. Thank you Carol, Lisa, Ilana and Daniella.

Thank you to my friends and every single yoga student who showed me we were all multidimensional beings and healing happened on so many levels.

Thank you to my past love's for showing me where the work was until I understood that all the ins and outs of love are part of the richness.

Thank you Mother Earth for the constant reminder that change happens and it just isn't that serious in the grand scheme of things.

Much love to you my reader. I wish you joy.
x Flea
Fiona Goldsmith

I took a little fairy and past childhood.
Shades of Pollyanna gladness and Tinkerbell light,
penny fountains and wishing wells,
four leaf clovers and magic spells,
and wishing on the first star.
There's a place for happy endings,
and I believe in timing perfect and will to win,
and I still cross my fingers for luck and for love
and I just know Mister Right will walk in.
He's just running late so to fill in the wait
I've been dating fancy frogs
while he is missing.

This is one of many filtered passages.

The children call this passage the introduction.

They want a beginning and frankly it doesn't bother us.

We have a compassion for human children and their grown up fantasies.

We don't laugh out loud at them.

It isn't our place to tell them there was never a beginning.

There is no real time.

The moments just drift backward and forward, of their own accord.

What they choose to call time is only spaces between dreams.

Everything is simpler than it seems.

I would like to offer a lily pad of possibility...
Where the future is far from dire...
Where heaven is where we are now...

Breathe.

Where things come together in unexpected ways...
and are not obvious until the last paragraph,
of just another chapter...
and retrospect will be the wonderful teacher.

Breathe.

You can white knuckle your way through
with fear, outrage and baited breath...
Or sit back and watch the antics and find bemused.

Breathe.

Where your thoughts explore the moss
between the righteous white and black
and suddenly many shades of grey seem obvious...
if you think a certain way.

Breathe.

And the great perhaps?
That we had no say in it at all
and witnessing is all we are here for.

Breathe.

THE MERMAID

When a new soul fell out of the stars,
land and mountains reached out tall to claim her...
but the ocean rolled in and caught the baby in her arms
and the child was forever of the waves.

Her eyes were blue of sky reflected water.
Her skin the tan of daily sun drenched sand.
She was of the light in which reflection caught her,
dancing on moonlit dewy nights.

Her father took her to the beach when she was very small.
Let her ride winged ponies and taught her how to swim.
He showed her secret gardens in rock pools hidden deep.
He held her tiny hand and she trusted him.

Five rocks deep and low beneath the water was the measure
of whether she was ready to swim alone.
In her father's eyes she shone.
Brave and braver she'd become
and the sea became her safety and her home.

There were warriors who stood on boards and conquered seas
when waves were fullest.
Our mermaid became a warrior too.

She kept her footing in wild winds.
Surrendered to what the day would bring.
She was accustomed to wild weather on land too.
She sparkled like glass rolled to shimmer's in the sand.
Her laughter blended with gull calls in the sky.
Below the surface was her wonder land.
This mermaid was connected to the rhythm of the tides.

She grew up and got caught up in the symphony of women
and she acted out what she'd seen them choose.
To be every body's everything.
She was a helping hand in anything,
and she was perfect at everything she'd do.
She was a role model, an artist, a musician.
She became a teacher, a heroine too...
and what's more she was always good
and she was patient because that's what good girl's do.

The mermaid married and had babies
and simply gave herself away.
She was last on her long, long list of love.
She grew pale with eyes faded like a grey day.
Her sparkle dimmed with a cry of not enough.

Not enough sleep
Not enough time

Not enough money
Not enough
Not enough love
Not enough trust
Not enough support
Not enough.

More and more she was last on the list
which was still getting longer and longer.
As tide and time again her own needs
were ignored and trodden.
As time and tide again her little heart was broken.
Until she was out of balance...
Until she had lost her ease...
This was to be the doorway to her lesson...
To find well-being from disease.

First she went the way of doctors
and she wasn't getting better,
Then she took the way of healers
and the healings wouldn't hold
She felt defeat and sparkle-less.
Confused and tired and powerless...
So she whispered to the earth spirits,
"Send me a sign."

The sky spoke of raindrops as a remedy for everything.
The wind spoke of flying with the energy of freedom.
The earth said "take my fruits and flowers and be nourished."
The sea said "it's time to come back to me."

She learnt to move from her souls quiet murmurings,
finding that intuition guided her...
She stopped listening to negativity,
and felt hopefulness come alive in her.
She ate foods the colour of rainbows
and felt her strength return and grow.
She soaked herself in sunlight
and it made her womb space glow.
She hugged trees and connected
to earth's wondrous rhythm.
She had to learn to receive love
to balance all the giving...
She trusted
deeply trusted and the cells of her mind responded.
And she loved,
Oh how she loved but now her own self was included...
and she was happy
oh so happy, and the gifts she had unfolded,
and the lesson was there was more to life
than being good and brave.
Just giggle with delight
and feel the healing of the wave.

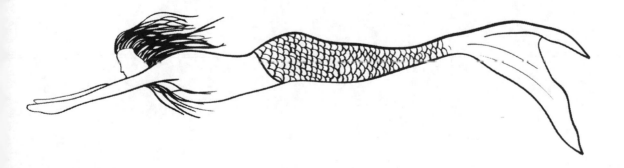

PURPOSE

"What is my purpose asked the possum to the sky?
I feel of little consequence when dingo's passing by.
I have not majesty of mountain, nor powerful raging sea,
So what really is the purpose of a little one like me?
A bull ant has the power to carry a world upon his back
and a wallaby can hop and pouch her young,
a wombat does the pace of zen
the tortoise halves that pace again...
She river carves her way through rocks
and wild ponies make grand tracks
with men up on their backs."

Possum gazed at her reflection
in the brown of billabong
unaware her little story was touching lives...
A word-weaving poet was inspired
in the dimming light
by Possum's mesmerizing beauty and shining eyes.

The gum tree whispered quietly in a rustle sound like wind,
"you are here to make a home in me
and keep babies safe within"
and the fruit trees sweet talked softly
in a sound like dropping leaves,
"It is you who feasts on apples and spreads our seeds."

"Ahh" said the Mother Earth
"worth depends not on your size
but your souls yearning.
The caterpillar transforms from crawling to flying thing
and the dusk to day keeps turning.
There is perfection and a purpose to everything,
every rock, every storm and every tree.
You are living your uniqueness each moment of your life
in my evolving tapestry,
until you too dissolve to dust and return to me."

Her reflection became beautiful when she was loved...
And ahh that was exquisite, addictive and powerful medicine.
But love had abandoned her before
and pain of that was as intolerable as it's presence was healing.

Like a desert bloom...
she had dried up slowly
and disengaged from her feelings to survive
the pain of not being enough.

Her lover was a surprise that arrived without expectation
and bought her back to life.
He unwrapped her like a puzzle and adored every part of her.
She felt rescued...
She felt potent, alive.
She beamed in the joy of connection.
And ahh that was exquisite.
There was fire in her heart again
and juice in secret places.

But attention faded ...
And she felt the fear rise.
She feared the drought again and more deeply now.
She thought she was not enough again.
She started to prepare for the pain and it was intolerable.
She began a strange behaviour of giving power
to what she feared most and it was creative.
She blamed the sunshine for too much light
and the rain for its absence.
She blamed her lover for less attention.
None of these things made love come back
the way it had been.

A desert flower does not wait for the rain to fall.
It simply exists.
Parched...

It dies.
When the rain has been missing for a long time
the flower does not focus on the absence
of the thrill of thunder…
She just is.
The full moon whispered.. "listen little saboteur…
Nature is the flow of seasons.
It can not be contained.
It must cycle.
Looking into the change…
Choose to see the beauty and the possibility
in each sacred season.
Surrender
and know powerfully that the rain will come again.
The love that you are
is not dependent on that."

The small brown Scribe tried to keep a diary of the children's adventures
but being both short sighted and easily distracted, it wasn't easy.
"The rare human child reading these stories
will remember being part of it all.
Most, at best will only enjoy the stories,
but perhaps that is enough!!"
She laughed, pleased to have discovered a brighter side.

She's uncomfortable in awkward.
The cracking of the shell.
The push-me-pull-you desire to grow out of a space
that is crammed...
Uncomfortable.
Not longer a fit.
Too small for who she is now.
She crawls
Reaches
Quick
Flighty
Unbalanced
with the practice of standing on her own feet.
She's growing a muscle of confidence
and no longer accepts defeat.
Have you seen her fullness?
Can you accept her wings unfolding?
Taking up space she didn't inhabit before?
Growth is assured
as she meets challenge with bravery.
The tears she's shed are not weakness.
Just an outward manifestation
of a release that leads to change.

REFLECTION

There's your face again reflected in still water.
Keep almost seeing you, in the distance in the crowd.
I hear the sound of laughter and I turn around to catch you,
but your daughter has got your eyes
and your son has kept your sound,
and I am caught again,
unexpectedly missing you.

Still see your flavours,
your scarlets and your golds etched in memory.
Cinnamon and musk,
scents of absent you and the comforts only temporary.

I hear your whisper in the calling of the winter.
The sweet coziness of memory when I'm snuggled by the fire.
I try to manifest you but I'm feeling into emptiness...
and the tears come for a while.
I miss your face
and again I'm unexpectedly missing you.

and again I'm unexpectedly missing you.
I miss your face
and the tears come for a while.
I try to manifest you but I'm feeling into emptiness...
The sweet coziness of memory when I'm snuggled by the fire.
I hear your whisper in the calling of the winter.

scents of absent you and the comforts only temporary.
Cinnamon and musk,
your scarlets and your golds etched in memory.
Still see your flavours,

unexpectedly missing you.
and I am caught again,
and your son has kept your sound,
but your daughter has got your eyes
I hear the sound of laughter and I turn around to catch you,
Keep almost seeing you, in the distance in the crowd.
There's your face again reflected in still water.

Kira was quiet of disposition,
small and closed and shy,
and she had practiced small for the longest time.
Kira lived in a castle,
where girls wore loud pigment and strong sound.
Where they strutted and swayed their hips
and were confident and proud.
But Kira was the whisper.
She was never quite the same,
and the louder the others were the quieter she became.

Listening is an art that only listeners perfect.
And Kira was an audience which made her different...
The rest were all performers so busy being heard
that they missed the subtle messages
within pause, tone and word.

Inspiration chose this time to interfere.
She sat on Kira's shoulder and whispered in her ear.
She said...
"Let's paint our pretty eyes.
See what this full moon brings.
Let's jump and ride on astral beams.
Let's scream and laugh and sing.
Let's pretend we're beautiful on our insides too
And act the way we want to feel
and practice till it's true.
And at the dot of mid night
dance like we own the floor.
In that magic moment
you will become the girl who roars!"

You are a flower
that although open and face forward to the sun,
still doesn't know it's magnificence.
So many layers yet to unfold,
past the possibilities of your imagination.
You are the fruit of the rose and the briar
that gives no hint to who you will be,
unless you plunge deep into the allowing.
There is so much more than your believing...
and your education...
There is not a preparation that can truly ready you
for your ravenous unfolding.
Owning all that turns up each day.
Letting go of blame, shame and opinion.
Intuition wants to flex and challenge you...
but feel into it.
Are you are charged with inspiration and joyful excitement?
Are you open to the noticing?
It's time to stop pushing against your tides.

ROSE

This is the story of a beautiful girl,
who fell to earth to stay and play for a while.
Her name was Rose.
Her cheeks were blush and her smile was wide.
Her golden hair spiraled down her back.
She held herself tall and light.
There was no doubt that she was a beauty.
Rose came to Earth on a beam of sunset,
at the close of a perfect day.
She came to learn a particular lesson.
A lifetime ago,
Rose had chosen the moment in time
and the unique story that would be hers.
The only problem was that upon arriving on Earth,
she could no longer remember the ending!

In her early years Rose simply merged with the life around her...
school, parties, home, friends and family.
Rose lost her self in loud music, computers, television, drama,
and busy, busy, busy!
She was happy.
Well she thought she was happy.

By the time she'd grown into a young woman,
Rose was so immersed in the busy, busy, busy
that she had completely forgotten who she was.
And there was always a voice in her head talking talk.
Even in the night when the world was quiet,
the voice was talking, talk, talk.
Rose no longer remembered a time when pauses
were comfortable spaces between things to do.

Rose's mind was full of a not so happy voice.
Worst of all,
Rose began to believe that she was the voice!
This voice was unkind and always finding things wrong.
So she thought she was wrong.
The voice was not brave and always sounding afraid,

so Rose was not quite brave and always somewhat afraid.
The voice kept talking, talk, talk
and Rose's head was spinning.
At this very moment,
a fairy was passing by.
She could hear the noisy, chaos in Roses mind
and decided it was time to intervene.
This fairy's mission was to teach that things
are not always as they seem.
Her name was Inspiration.
Inspiration flew onto Rose's left shoulder
and whispered softly in her ear.

"What is wrong, sweet Rose?" She inquired.
"I think and I think
and I know exactly what's wrong with me.
My nose is too big" said Rose.
When Rose looked in the mirror, all she could see
was a gigantic nose.
"My face is all nose," she said quietly.
"How awful it is to be so ugly!
I think and I think and my heart skips a beat,
because I know what others think of me.
They talk about the girl with the incredible nose.
I know I will never be good enough.
With a nose like this, who would ever love me?"
The more Rose thought,
the more she was sure, something was wrong with her,
and the more unhappy she became.

"What are you here for
Rose of the Sunset?" Inspiration asked.
"What am I here for?" murmured Rose, almost sleep talking.
"Am I here to be an astronaut, a dancer, or a sailor?
Am I meant to tame wild elephants or be a famous writer?
Is my destiny in music, making movies, or planting gardens..."

Feeling vexed and hopeless, Rose choked back tears,
"This, is all anyone ever sees.
With a nose like this, what is there for me to be?"

Since Rose of the Sunset could not see
past the end of her nose,
she assumed that everyone else saw what she saw.

Inspiration whispered,
"Rose, it's time to find the quiet within you again.
It's time to stop listening to that voice inside your head
that you think is you,
and find out who you really are!
Here's how you start.
Take a long slow deep breath.
Now slowly let the breath flow out all the way,
more completely than you usually do.
And then wait."

Rose of the Sunset listened carefully to Inspiration
and took a long slow deep breath in.
Rose let her breath flow out and out... and waited.
To her surprise the breath came back in,
slowly and gently, all by itself.
After another long breath out and again,
the gentle breath returned.
Rose's body began to feel as if it were breathing itself.
Each breath in seemed to happen of its own accord...
naturally, soothingly,
And then something amazing happened.
Everything was quiet for the first time she could remember.
There was no voice in her head talking talk talk.
Instead there was a big open space inside her.
Her body relaxed with her breathing and it felt wonderful.
She literally felt like she was expanding
and getting taller at the same time.
Rose let herself relax into the moment

and she felt quite different!
Maybe even a little happy!

Rose felt so good after that
and the good feeling lasted for half a day.
She tried the same thing the next day…and the next.
Soon every day Rose would sit down somewhere
and let her body gently breathe itself.

Day by day Rose felt herself changing.
She found herself seeing… into the distance,
below the surface,
into the eyes and the hearts of others.
She saw the shimmer in the leaves of the trees,
the sparkle in the eyes of insects,
and the curved edge of the world were the earth
reaches the sky in absolutely every direction.
She found herself hearing…
the sweet chatter of the birds, the soft call of the breeze,
the droplets of rain on the sidewalk,
the messages below the words,
and the gentle harmony hidden in nature.
Soon she was hearing
the deep hum that was beneath it all.

As Rose came to her senses,
she began to breathe in the perfumes of the Earth…
the inky sweet night,
the ancient salts of seas carried on loving breezes,
and the honeyed scent flowing from each of thousands of flowers,
each one adding joy and riches to her world.
Rose began to feel
the touch of the breeze as it caressed her cheek
and combed unruly curls into her hair.
She found herself noticing the tiniest drop of rain,
the sun's radiance on her skin
and damp moss beneath her bare toes.
Each touch was a sweet hello from the new friends
she was making in the silent world.
Each taste grew deeper and clearer.

and every time Rose ate, she felt more alive.
She began to know that her body's simple longing for certain colours
and tastes were a way to heal and care for herself.
She began to understand what she desired, was what she needed.
Rose began to trust herself.
Day by day, she continued to take time and let her body breathe itself.
Rose continued to change.
She began to feel her blood flowing, her heart beating,
her body taking in the food and water that nourished her,
the living pulsing aliveness that that was Rose.
She felt connected to the life in every living thing
and in the world around her.

Gradually over the weeks of quiet breathing,
it dawned on Rose
that the voice in her head was no longer there,
not even in the midst of a busy day.
Instead, she was watching, hearing, smelling, tasting and feeling.
Rose was being.
The voice was not there and Rose still was!
What a surprise!
The voice was not Rose at all!

Just then Rose caught a reflection in the mirror
of a beautiful girl.
As she smiled a welcome, at this lovely stranger
she was shocked to discover
the stranger was her own reflection.
She was the beautiful girl staring back at her.

Rose looked into the eyes,
into her very own eyes—and all at once she knew.
She had been a twinkle in the eye of a majestic leopard,
and she had been a tiny kangaroo rat.
She had been a witch doctor with eyes deep as night,
and a shimmer in the soul of a rainbow.

Stardust was what she was made of.
She was part of the Earth
and part of many other places.
And what's more…
everyone around her was made
of the same beautiful sparkling stuff that she was
and so was the buzzing gorgeous world.

In that moment Rose's heart opened completely,
like her namesake the rose.
And suddenly she remembered the ending of her story!

Learning to love her self
was the lesson she had come to Earth to learn.
This was her dream and destiny.
Rose finally knew all her layers of beautiful.
No one else could be Rose of the Sunset.
She was complete, special and perfect
in every way, exactly as she was.

She weeps.

Her flowing into lakes and rivers.

seas swell

skies pour...
And her deep ground waters pulse **and rise.**

She is neither sadness or ecstasy
in her perpetual cycle...
She is the seasons...
Indefinite
Circulating
Source
Inconstant in everything but change.

Steaming jungles
Molten rocks
Parched barren red and gold deserts.
Her deep fires
Explode through cracks and fissures
Only hinting at the power within.
She thunders

and her skies crack in lighting

She coos

into winters and soft falls

She moans

and ice sheets tumble into oceans

She dreams and species pass away
And another born...
Ahhhh
and her ghosts are the everything of inspiration!

Like a caterpillar
ready to transform.
She wrapt herself in deep protection,
resting down into discomfort...

In any awakening there is struggle.
Birthing of the new...
Imagination suspects it's getting worse,
Exhaustion overwhelms...
And finally there is exposed
raw new flesh
and stretching wet wings,
awesome in their fragility and possibility.
An entirely new creature is born.

There's a special kind of sunshine...
Seeps from your inside out...
A golden glowing knowing
that it will all work out...

Even if you can't imagine
who or how or why???
Even if the overwhelm
brings tear bursts to your eyes.

Below that there's the comfort
that we are just wave riding...
Almost drowning is the place
the cup of change is hiding.
With in a star we wished upon
we will one day see
that this was always perfect timing...

Let go.
Give in.
The flow is within...
Let heart stuff guide us!
We can not grasp the mystery
until we have danced in time
with time behind us.

Ahh we are in a wave right now
visiting the undertow...
and it's deep here...
No longer playing
superficially in the shallows...
let's find our inner dolphin
and come up for air together.

And we know,
deep inside we know,
it's going to be alright
because change is the promise
and the mother cycles...

There's sun behind those roaring waves
and storm clouds
and dolphins laughter on the other side.

O was dipped in gorgeousness from the day she came.
Lit up from with in
her wide cheeky smile made dragons tame.
She could brighten night skies with hopefulness.
Her laughter could soften storms
and when she broke out into song every heart was hers.
And the trees leaned in to hear her.
Dolphins danced when she was near.
She spoke dog and cat and unicorn.
Holding all hearts equal,
all hearts dear.

The spell that O cast made small souls feel grand,
as large as a palace,
infinite as sand.
So truly O loved.
So truly she cared.
We were kissed by her sunshine and blessed when she's there.
Her every night time dreaming's became our sweet reality
as she held softly to her visions till the dawn
and when the morning sun
kissed the window sills
her dreams became real and flew off into morning.

And O how she loved and her love created family.
And O how we loved her and she gave us precious memories.
O led by example dispensing hope and love and laughter;
positive that the world will spin into happy ever after
and because she was so positive
of course it was.

Eyes shuttered in glimpses before dawn...
when there are words floating through her mind,
begging capture.
Lyrical,
textured,
a complete sound bite
that seems to have written itself.
In those moments
where chaos has settled into knowing,
and lessons have been painfully understood,
she gets to quickly inscribe words to paper.
She has learnt to get out of the way
and to accentuate the pause....
where ahhhaaa turns up corners
and hmmmm dives deep.
Rest, repair and inspiration
gifted by sleep.

On a golden day when I focus on my plenty...
I slide into the essence of magical.
riding luck and laughter,
Feeling lovely and loving
into opportunity...
and the noticing of the better feeling flowing...
and choosing to follow that.
And when my gaze slips...
my mood dips...
to lack or loss, to lonely or poor me
worry, obsession, judgement or negativity...
all energy goes there overwhelmingly.
and my shoulders roll forward and smile forgets.
Amazing is my power
to wish up spaces for my car...
To run energy through my hands.
To take the shimmering
gorgeous lit up goddess out to play...
Strange how I forget all that
on a silver day.

BIG LOVE

In order to be good
she must go last on a long list
which ended in the feeling of crumpled brown paper.
She had tried and tired of giving herself away
and still there was a silence inside that was emptiness.
Life had been a balance between giving everything
and searching for something to fill her,
to make her soul complete.
She looked for it everywhere
Without really knowing where, what, why??
Ahhh but in the quiet....
in the silence she gave herself she fell deeply into love.
As she practiced random acts of loving herself...

Love flowered.
Love healed old stories of not enough.
Love saw through her eyes and her shadows danced.
Love made her skin prickly alive in music.
Love made strangers no longer strange.
Love made everyone special.
Love wrapped its arms around loneliness **making it sacred.**
Love smelt like flowers and tempted like **hot chocolate.**
Love sat quietly with friends.
The love that was within her flowed over
and touched everything she touched
and little healings happened everywhere.
Love was the door
she had not realized she was looking for
and loving herself was turning the key.

We are of nature
passing through the spectrum of weather,
from calm to raging seas...
and always there is brightness
behind clouds changing constantly.
And yes there are things we can not control,
pretty much everything...
As we tumble with the tempests
both changed and born again.
Even the most intense experiences mutate in time...
Always the possibility of evolution
or staying stuck on the ride again...
and then comes a moment you can surrender...
"No hands mum!"
I'm no longer holding on.

Her intuition rises
with a quiet voice in her heart
Go slow today my love...
walk mindfully on your path.
There's treasures hidden for you
in places you could miss...
Look for beauty in the shadows
and sweet clues in the distance.
Look deeper into faces.
Feel energy of words.
There is magic that's not hidden
but only obvious to those who slow down time.
Trust your body's path to wisdom.
She speaks inconvenient truths.
Connecting you to ebb and flow
and feeling fragile is both a story and a clue.
So honour how you are today
and rest
rather than push through.

What to make of these scary strange times?

The fairies had a shelf life
of two hundred years or more
and even they had never seen times like these before.
The humans were in lock down.
Full of upset and fight.
They were confined to their homes and curfew every night.
The wisdom fairy gurgled...
Her laughter touched the sky
and woke up sleepy crawling things
and butters flying by.

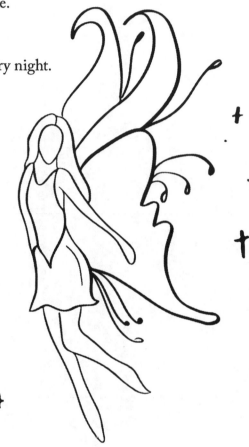

It's time to get to know themselves
without stress and manic pace.
See other sides of everything.
To slow and hibernate.

There many more than one truth
and the maybes in between.
Perspectives change through dew drops.
For some time is what you need.

Things are neither as they sound
or even as they seem...
This is your cocoon you are pushing through,
the winter of your dreams.
Haha she giggled
It's not meant to be easy...
Might as well enjoy the ride.

A wobbly fledgeling
on the edge of possibility.
Hesitant.
Too comfortable in discomfort.
He'll take a risk
over living in cotton wool,
over the limited cosiness of knowing...
Average is a little luke warm
for his taste...
He's getting good at brushing off
and try, try, try again...
Preferring the stretch toward greatness
with the possibility of falling!
If he leaps
there's jagged cliffs
and a treacherous descent...
But he chooses to hold the vision
of being picked up by the wind... Tumbling into the horizon
and Flying...

The bear didn't dazzle you like a dragon.
He didn't mesmerize.
The bear did not bewitch or teach you to fly.
But you fell into green eyes
which didn't match his woolly face.
Cool green eyes
always looking to another far off place.
This bear just loved to hug you most
when you looked surprised
And you felt small and warm in his arms
and lost in his beautiful eyes.
He was a big bear with a small cubs smile
that he didn't use enough.
He watched a fairy child for a long while
and he slowly fell in love.
And when he was with her he caught her laughter
and she had to be kissed.
And all he hoped for was a happy ever after
that could not exist.
Bears and bubbles are different creatures
too far apart.
They played a while in secret gardens
and the bear lost his heart.

46

On the secret silent thoughts of a bubble...
Can I say I love you in a way?
In a special small way can we care Mr Bear?
Can we stay a while?
I hope you want to play a while?
In a special small way can we share Mr Bear?
One touches softly on something lovely while it's living
to keep a precious memory.
Let's just take it as it comes Mr Bear.
"You've been kissed," he said
and she wanted to thank him for that.
She tried so hard to tell him with her eyes
but the moment was gone like so many silent thank you's.
Bears and Bubbles float on air and walk in secret gardens.
You can have it while its there Mr Bear.
As long as you smile,
we smile even for a short while.
We can have a lovely time together Mr Bear.

INTO THE UNEXPECTED

Treading water
in uncertainty...
Turning fear into excitement
is challenging alchemy...
And it's okay to feel challenged
by the constant and relentless,
when ease is a but memory
in the far away of distance...
But nature reminds us
with explosive flowering of spring
that change is guaranteed
and we will rise again.

Pleasure
Hmmmmmm
Heart murmurs, races, beats and speaks,
solar plexus flutters,
womb warms and gut churns,
skin recognizes excellence,
with hairs standing to alert attention.
Skin on skin.
Tongue, lips, wet kisses.
Hmmmmmmm
Eyes feasting on beautiful.
Every direction of beautiful.
Bodies, eyes and trees
crumbling mountains
and distant lands in cloud
and the oh so very small...
The detail, texture,
where patterns merge and meet,
and sweet birds chatter,
winds caress a cheek.
Ocean and night skies,
eyes magnetized by eyes,
Souls witnessed in a dream.
Ah yes beauty is a feast
Hmmmmmmm

Sweet lady Alice
was always in love on the full moon.
She'd lose her balance,
distracted by smiles
she'd love too soon.
And that's what she'd say
and it sounded ok when she said it.
But when she'd think in retrospect,
when the moon had less effect
she'd regret it.
Taken by the moment
she would declare her adoration,
but with the light of day
she'd feel less infatuation.
With the dawn of the sun
she'd moan "What have I done?'
They called her the fickle fairy
in the puddles and moss
as they listed the princes
that she's loved and lost.

Said sweet lady Alice
In a soft fairy voice,
"There are so many princes
I just can't make a choice.
I am distracted by smiles
and I feel myself straying.
I am flirting with danger,
that's what fairy town's saying.
But I will dance with them
all while they're here to enjoy
I have too much love for a single boy!"

INSPIRATION

Ho hum, ho hum there's work to be done.
Inspiration sat quietly on the window sill.
The wide-eyed adventurer waited patiently,
until Tasha's sleepy eyes found her.

"Who's there? What's going on?" whispered the child.

"Shhhh, I have only come to see you"
the little fairy told her firmly with her eyes.

"Are you a dream?" whispered Tasha staring at a tiny person.
Her heart was beating so fast
she thought she might have been having a heart attack.
Perhaps she was she thought,
wrapping her arms around herself in panic.

"Hush now, it is time to lie back and listen"
the fairy commanded.
"It is time for you to learn how the universe works.
I have come to share the first rule with you, Tasha."

So Tasha pulled the blankets up to her chin.
Her brown eyes absorbing the little being
with a very large personality.
"Who are you? You don't exist. You're probably a dream"
said Tasha with attitude.

"Do I feel real Tasha?" soothed Inspiration
as a warm glow spread from the little fairy
wrapping them both in a cocoon of pink.
Tasha found herself dropping down into softness and sweet calm.
The fairy spoke clearly with out raising her voice.
She spoke straight into the child's mind.

"Now crunch every part of your body starting at your toes.
Tense all your muscles tight...
your fists, your legs, your shoulders, your face...
hold everything with tension...
for as long as you can with out turning blue...
and then completely release.

Allow relaxation to feel like melting.
When you really relax, notice yourself filling up and expanding."
crooned the little fairy in a voice like music.
"Quiet your mind...listen with your senses.
Feel my words in your skin, your nose, your mouth, your fingers and toes,
but mostly in your heart,
because inside your heart you will recognize what it true for you.
Relax and listen Tasha. It is time.
My Name is Inspiration and I am your souls gift to you.
I am your connection to your inner wisdom
until you know your own way.
I have come to you because you have been losing your way
and there are things you need to understand.
So lie back, connect and take in the sound of my voice,
the birds chirping, the tree's rubbing their branches together,
the airplane buzzing in the sky.
Listen to the sound of your breathing.
Feel your heart pumping energy around and through
the mystery's of your body.
Can you hear the quiet snoring of the cat,
the dripping of the tap,
the sounds of family waking up in other rooms?
Can you expand your listening
to include the traffic in the distance,
the laughter of big kids kicking balls in the street?
Keep listening and expanding the listening
until you can feel it growing out through your ears.
Imagine and immerse yourself.
This moment is full. Let yourself feel it."

Tasha's eyes got wider and she waited...
feeling some excitement in the fluttering of her heart.

"So here is the first lesson." Inspiration paused
and the birds were quiet as if they too were waiting.

"You are perfect in every single way Tasha.
You are perfect just the way you are, right now.
You are special and whole and complete.
You don't have to be better because you already are better.
You are beautiful inside and outside Tasha...
but you need to know that you are totally creative.

Your thoughts create your world.
If you think the day is wonderful it is.
If you think it is boring, you create with less energy
and make it drab and unexciting.
That is how it works.
It is not what actually happens that counts
but how you think about what happens
that creates your moments" explained Inspiration.
"I do not understand" said Tasha.
"Okay" laughed the fairy "you have two buckets of sand,
full to the same level...about half way,
and a happy soul describes the bucket a half full
and a grumpy souls says it is half empty.
Who is right Tasha?"
"They are both right" said the child with a cheeky grin.
"But who is happier?" said Inspiration.
"Neither because they both only have half!" laughed Tasha.
"Maybe...
but maybe the one who can be happy with what they have got is the happiest!
The point is in the choosing.
There is not one reality Tasha. Every day we choose our reality.
We choose how we respond to the circumstances that occur.
We make choices and define our experience every moment.
When you think happy thoughts, your body responds by making happy chemicals,
which feel like tickles from the inside.
When you plant a smile on that lovely face
the world tends to smile back at you. That is how it works!

So back to Tasha being perfect in every way." smiled Inspiration.
"Well I am not" said Tasha pushing out a stubborn bottom lip.
"Enough of that. Just listen" flowed Inspiration.
"Here is Tasha, brown eyed, gorgeous and talented.
She is perfect. Compared to whom?
There are no others like Tasha. She is unique and special.
If she choses to think of herself as less, it doesn't make it true.
It is just a thought, but it not a helpful and supportive thought.
None of us is really better or worse than anyone else.
How can you compare? Each person is a petal of uniqueness evolving.
Each child is individual, special
and has their own beauty, magic and destiny.

Your duty is to become yourself
and the best possible self you can be is happy.
You won't be full of joy all the time.
There will always be difficult situations.
Your mother will yell sometimes
and your father will always want you to tidy your room
until it is actually done.
What you need to understand is that no one can take your happiness,
your joy or your sense of self away from you.
You have to give it away."
They both stared at the bright stars winking from the heavens,
listening to the birds chattering outside the window.

"No one makes you mad Tasha.
You must choose to be angry.
You could choose something else.
You could try on cheeky or wise, mature or ridiculous.
You just need to know that you are doing the choosing.
How you respond to your life is always up to you,
every time and every day.
Choosing is your power and your magic.
Remember being grumpy finds reasons for being grumpy.
Expecting difficult will find difficult.
Feeling small or less does not make it so
but it does not make you feel good either." Soothed the little fairy.
"Choosing to be happy and wearing your smile on the inside,
you gives you a rosy glow that other people can't help catching.
Your light ignites a spark in others because energy is infectious.
Your joy keeps coming back at you in laughter
and the eyes of others."

Happy for every and no particular reason.
Not because things are rolling out perfectly,
but because life's humour is bubbling up anyway.
Riding a tide that feels new and fresh and mine...
full of adventure...
Pockets of promise.
I am doing and being in sync.
Traveling, evolving and even witnessing the process
as I let go of the oars and let change be....
With timing divine
without knowing where I am going
I'm flying free.
Hello joy, for no particular reason.

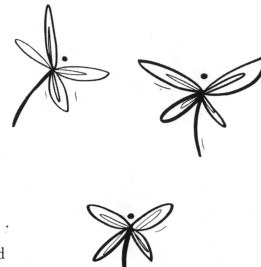

Just dancing with air,
fleeting moon light affair,
had me smiling at everything.
Neither finished not started,
beware turning half hearted,
the ride was bewildering.
Fun and games got out of hand,
too big brown eyed to understand
that he didn't say what he meant.
Broke the spell I was under
as I started to wonder
where my cheeky friend went.
Suggesting just to be fair,
Protesting handle with care
Requesting tell me if you've cooled of me.
Because we can friends,
just depends how it ends,
please don't let me make a fool of me.
But distance had to say it.
You stalled and I waited
and only the silence didn't lie.
And all I have to say about your going away
is that you promised to say goodbye.
Please come home Morgan,
I am terribly something without you.
All is forgiven,
Yours sincerely the fairy Scribe.

Once there was a little prince
who ran away from home
to live a life of fun and games
far from the family throne.
He threw away his golden crown.
and slipped through the gates of fairy town,
to dance round toad stools in a ring
and fairy songs he learnt to sing.
He slept under blankets of fallen leaves.
He played in secret gardens.
He learnt the language of the bees.
The butterflies were his friends.
One day the king and queen he missed,
so fairy town goodbye he kissed,
and through the little town he sped
until he reached his little bed.
He woke to find he'd never been
and fairy town was just a dream.
He woke up on the same day he had gone.
But in his little hand he found a **tiny silver fairy** pound.
He had something left to wish **upon.**

Come to me lonely when the world puts you down.
I'll pick up the pieces my poor little clown.
Bring me faded pantomimes,
it won't take me a while,
to sew all your bells back on and paint on your smile.

Come to me lonely when you're hurting inside.
I'll give you fairy floss and somewhere to hide.
And when ever lonely you should lose your way
I'll draw a map for you and send you back to play.

I'm the one you run to when you're feeling the need,
and when you're back together I am the one you leave.
And sometimes I feel lonely too as you walk out the door.
your smile back in place again
like a thousand times before.

Once there was a rainbow soul named Maria,
whose role in this lifetime
was to reflect back the truest colors of everyone she met
because that is all she saw.

She looked upon strangers and immediately loved them,
and through her eyes they saw their own deeply hidden beauty.
She saw past the habits and behavior of friends
and reflected their unique majesty,
and each one wanted to gather around her table
where she liked to nourish them
with food made with thoughtfulness
and her throaty laugh, her warm embrace and her bubbling love.

Maria was a revolution in pictures.
She was bold and inspired.
She made imagery to save the world.
She was the voice of the hidden and the quiet.
She absolutely knew what she was here for,
and she had a heart so big that loss touched her deeply
and joy was pure bliss.

My attraction to chanting and fire's a clue...
or the trees I whirl around under the moon,
and my love of herbal tonics and brews?
Hmmmmm

Inside there's a spirit, a sister to wild,
who taught my body to dance as a child...
And though I forgot to connect to the wind
and got tangled in stories on a journey within...
There's a part that was always a believer in magic
Hmmmmm

I had to the re-find the freedom I had lost.
to laugh with the magpies and commune with the dogs.
As I watched myself move from uptight to release.
I found myself wanting to play and to teach..
Hmmmmm

I'm loving the parts
that turned like the weather.
Both the calm and the turbulence merging together.
Tears and the giggles, the drama, the flirt.
The one that creates from the lessons she's learnt.
The heart that's been broken and come back for more.
The shadows that danced when no longer ignored.
And the mirror that finally understood
it was always my reflection I was seeing...
Hmmmmm

So I love this woman I have become
who rises in anger
and subsides into calm...
Who doesn't hold grudges,
and learns from mistakes.
Who enjoys all the parts of this life she creates...
Perhaps I'm a witch?
Hmmmmm

Printed in the United States
By Bookmasters